T0374111

VISIONS AND VERSE...
ALONG THE PATH

KAREN WALLACE

Copyright © 2020 by Karen Wallace. 819161

All rights reserved. No part of this book may be reproduced
or transmitted in any form or by any means, electronic
or mechanical, including photocopying, recording, or
by any information storage and retrieval system, without
permission in writing from the copyright owner.

The views expressed in this work are solely those of the author
and do not necessarily reflect the views of the publisher, and
the publisher hereby disclaims any responsibility for them.

To order additional copies of this book, contact:
Xlibris
844-714-8691
www.Xlibris.com
Orders@Xlibris.com

ISBN: Softcover   978-1-6641-3053-1
          Hardcover   978-1-6641-3054-8
          EBook   978-1-6641-3052-4

Library of Congress Control Number: 2020917641

Print information available on the last page

Rev. date: 09/19/2020

Introduction

As you view this collection, give yourself the gift of being present in the moment with each piece.

Allow yourself to hear the rhythm of the words and feel the energetic
flow of the colors and content in the paintings.

Many who have viewed the paintings and read the poems have wept, laughed out
loud, smiled with knowing, and felt a connection "like being there before."

This work is an expression of the string theory of quantum creativity, the universal
one, the thread of energy that runs through us all—past, present, and future!

This collection has been a gift to me, which I now joyfully share with the reader/viewer.

Honor to your path!

For Raven, who held the gate
open and the lantern high until
I could see the path.
Gratitude!

Lodgepole Pines

High in the mountains
A stand of lodgepole pines reaches for the sky
Evergreen boughs graceful in the breeze
A nest tucked into the branches
Deer graze nearby; a watchful cougar cruises through
An eagle soars overhead

Timber trucks shifting gears break the silence
The roar of chainsaws fills the air
A thousand years of growth crashes to the earth
Stripped of limbs, bark, and birds
Loaded onto a railroad car
Sawed, painted, tarred, and shingled
A small grass area, trees, shrubs, and flowers planted
A child and a dog play chase
And overhead an eagle soars

Karen Wallace

MESSENGER

A Gift from Teotihuacan

A gift from Teotihuacan, powerful and strange
A gift from the universe that knows no range
To be one with the stars, a gift far and wide
Where has my light gone, except by God's side?
A shattered assemblage point
Thank you, Great Spirit!
I shan't turn a deaf ear
I continue to hear it

The whishing of energy flying so fast

No need to remember distant thoughts from the past

Joyful surrender—freedom at last

Karen Wallace

TIME BETWEEN TIMES

Raven at Mitote

Raven chants at the mitote fire, the stars shine bright and glistening
The chant resounds a steady pulse, the universe quietly listening
The smoke unfurls and rises high, the embers glowing red
As I watch and listen, a golden halo softly surrounds his head

Dream, awaken, and dream again, a rhythm worth repeating

For visions gifted at the fire are often never fleeting

Karen Wallace

LAST OF THE
DOG MEN

A Shift . . . The Pale Wolf

The pale wolf is silent; she watches, and she waits

When Spirit begins to move, she quickens her hefty gait

She's breathing and feeling and open to change

Holding space for new energy and broadening her range

With eyes and ears on full alert

Her nose to the wind, her feet kick up dirt

She races forward; her intent is clear

Whatever she's after, she's showing no fear

Across the meadow and up the hillside

As she runs, she lets go of fear and of pride

As I watch, not too distant, my heart is filled with glee

Am I watching this wolf? Or is she one with me?

Karen Wallace

TALE FOR THE TRAIL

Wild Horses

Mustangs or brumbies, they don't care what we call them
They are horses! Wild horses! They know who they are
From deserts, mountains, and plains, no matter how far
Size does not matter. What color? Who cares!
It's the attitude that makes a difference, whether stallions or mares
When they whinny, ears perked, nostrils flared wide
And a mare brings her foal to show off with such pride
You know it's a wild one when you meet eye to eye
There's a presence, a knowing, a connection that flies
With beauty and splendor and spirit well known
You know what I mean if you've ever been thrown
Horses, wild horses! They reflect, often poignantly, our past
Our future hinges, in so many arenas, on helping them last

Karen Wallace

WHITE BUFFALO
DAWN

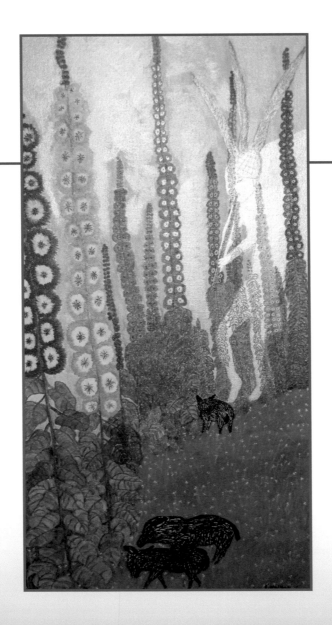

Hollyhocks and Javalenas

Hollyhocks and Javalenas along the border, don't you know

On the road out of Terlingua, where awesome wild things grow

They are fed by spirits long since past, whose essence lingers still

The road is long and winding, inviting songs at will

With windows down and hair blown back, a smile on my face

Breathing in the countryside, it's filled with simple grace

People of the earth live here and have since ancient times

Legends speak of travelers from the South communicating with music and signs

The Hollyhocks and Javalenas remember . . . macaw feathers, a flute, and a mime

Karen Wallace

LONG ROAD HOME

Firestorm

A fox spies a red-shafted flicker in the forest
"I am coming to get you, hey hey, ho ho"
"You'll never catch me; you are way too slow"
"My sight is set; I am crouching low"
"Such a funny furry beast; he makes me laugh
Just one little hop, and the wings are aft"
Then the wind shifts with a mighty draft
"Whew! What was that? It came so fast"
"It roared like a train, with a fiery blast"
"Did you see it?"
"I don't know"
"Where did it come from?"
"Where did it go?"
"Are we still here, or should we mourn?"
"Only spirits survive a firestorm"
"Let's go together back to the stars"
"This time I think we should visit Mars"

Karen Wallace

LABOR OF LOVE

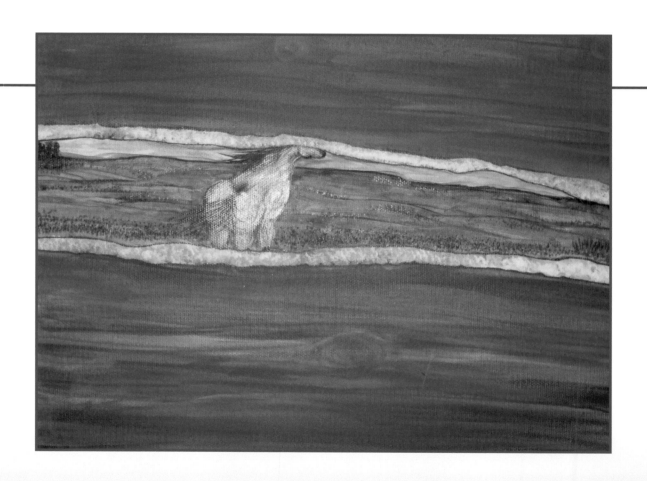

Puma

Puma in the desert, silhouette at sunset, orange backlight on clouds, dark shadow enhanced
Quietly crouching low, stalking Spirit perchance?
Long and sleek, low and slow through the cactus and Joshua trees
A predator, yellow eyes fixated, moves forth with stealth and with ease
She's watching and waiting, perfect place, perfect time
Patient and curious, sincere with intent—make the energy mine!
Puma medicine is powerful like the wind, wild and free
Come sit by the fire, mitote dreaming with me
No time to be timid when you are chasing the light
Step up! Race forward! Embrace it with all your might!
Walk the labyrinth at sunset, accompanied by a Tibetan bowl and a fife
Engage with sincerity, open doors in this life

Karen Wallace

FOX TROT

Spark!

Spark! What is it?
Is it why the time flies?
Spark is the essence
That shines in the eyes
The whisper, the promise
Of Spirit to find
When it is least expected
And far from the mind
It dwells in the spirit
Deep-seated and real
The breath of a baby
The hiss of an eel
The roar of a lion
The click of a heel
Not symbols, not time frames
Not boats, planes, or cars
Spark is the pathway
From Titicaca to Mars

Karen Wallace

EAGLE'S GIFT

Shadows

Celebrate the shadows as you journey from day into night
A gift awaits inside the shadows, vision open to insight
Vision is where it starts, then mind and soul fall in
Perception makes a mighty shift as integrity begins
Pay attention along the edges, where it turns from light to dark
That is the space where dreamtime flows and tranquility embarks
So stay alert, be wise and kind, and always do your best
Shadows, where the details lie, will put you to the test

Karen Wallace

SPOOKED

The Pearl

The mollusk is a humble sort
Not given to ovatious purport
Enjoying a quiet life under the sea
Until confronted with a grain of adversity
Then softly and slowly, the mollusk awakes
And gives undivided attention for as long as it takes
Until smooth and luminous replaces gritty irritation
It's like birthing an infant who has no limitations
Human eyes stare in awe and wondrous delight
To truly admire the quiet beauty of a pearl, such an incredible sight
What a role model for working with adversity
That's how I want my life to be!

Karen Wallace

SHORT CUT TO
THE DREAMTIME

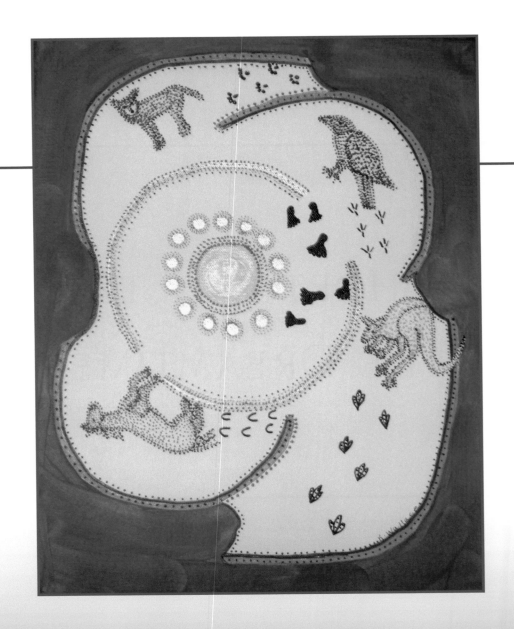

A Tribute to Aboriginal Dreamtime

Come with me, please take my hand

To the Red Centre, Australia's Outback, Arnhem Land

Dreamtime flows at Uluru, the people's sacred site

Wall paintings tell of mysteries handed down with all their might!
Dreamtime paintings must come from the heart
Reflect your own story, no secondhand art

Take your time, tell your tale of how you got to where

Ride a camel or a brumby, take the Ghan; if all else fails, fly in by air

Of course, you can go by walkabout like Aboriginal people do

Just keep in mind, *they* know the way, and of course, who can marry who

Who is who and what is what, no written language required

Set your intent, don't tell yourself lies—what you find out *is* what you desired

Karen Wallace

SPIRIT TEE PEES

Rides with a Feather

Rides with a feather
A friend for all time
Fierce and ruthless with pretense
In particular, mine
Rides with a feather
Tied in her hair
Rides not a stallion
But a sturdy gray mare
Truth is her mantra
No time for dismay
Truth *is* the mantra
Show me the way
Back from the stars with me
Riding on high
With her on my left shoulder
How fortunate, I

Karen Wallace

Betrayal:
Sand Creek

She Dances until the Sun Rises

Ceremony! Ceremony! Ceremony!
The drum begins at dusk
Steady rhythm, steady rhythm
Calling, encouraging, enticing
Hair hangs loose to her waist
Arms swing high in the air
Hands clap, silver bangles jangle
Long gauze skirt sways around bare feet
Swirling in the dirt around the fire
Dark the night, Mars aglow
Circling the blazing logs
Chanting positive energy grows alive
Pink line kisses the horizon
The shimmering sphere begins the climb

Karen Wallace

Printed in the United States
By Bookmasters